The Colors of Leadership & Management

Understanding management styles through the eyes of personality types

George J. Boelcke, FCI

Also by George Boelcke:

- Colorful Personalities: Discover Your Personality Type Through the Power of Colors
- Colorful Personalities: Audio CD
- The Colors of Leadership and Management
- The Colors of Parent and Child Dynamics
- The Colors of Relationships
- Colors Tools for Christians
- It's Your Money! Tools, Tips and Tricks to Borrow Smarter and Pay It Off Quicker US - Spanish & Canadian Editions (www.yourmoneybook.com)

To Contact the Author:

George Boelcke facilitates seminars throughout North America for companies and organizations ranging from Fortune 500 firms to small businesses, church groups, relationship seminars, conventions and schools. George can be contacted:

By e-mail: george@vantageseminars.com
Via web-site: www.vantageseminars.com
By mail: U.S.: 14781 Memorial Dr. #1183, Houston, TX 77079
Canada: Box 4080, Edmonton, AB T6E 4S8

Library and Archives Canada Cataloguing in Publication

Boelcke, George J., 1959–
    The colors of leadership & management: understanding management styles through the eyes of colors / George J. Boelcke. — 2nd ed.

Includes index.
ISBN-13: 978-0-9736668-3-0

    1. Executives—Psychology. 2. Leadership—Psychological aspects.
    3. Color—Psychological aspects. I. Title.
    II. Title: Colors of leadership and management.

    HD57.7.B63 2006   658.4'094   C2006-902241-0

Design assistance: David Macpherson
Layout & typeset by: Ingénieuse Productions, Edmonton, AB
Edited by: Lisa Reimche
Printed and Bound in the United States of America

Contents

Leaders influence others.
But in much different ways —
long before they actually get a title.

For any leader, an in-depth understanding of Colors in the workplace is a powerful resource. It is an indispensable tool to increase teamwork, boost morale, reduce stress, improve communication and affect productivity. It becomes part of the culture and vocabulary, while putting words with feelings and creating an understanding of the link in our personality types between motives, recognition and behaviors. It also impacts your staff's thinking and judgments, with a measurable impact on relationships with bosses, co-workers and customers.

Survey after survey continues to show that around 60 to 80 percent of people are not happy in their jobs. Yet in the vast majority of situations, using the tools of understanding personality types will have an immediate impact on this figure. Just a slightly different management approach, a few minor changes in dealings with staff, or change in job description, can significantly and measurably change this statistic.

After all, isn't the goal to retain valuable staff? Isn't it more practical and smarter to do a little more of what works and a little less of what doesn't, especially in an environment where retention of staff is becoming more and more of an issue? But it starts with being able to learn and understand that each personality type almost speaks a different language. How sad, that the average company continues to invest less than three percent of their training budget on front-line staff and very few management teams are trained in using the practical and powerful tools of understanding personality types.

"In my years studying leadership and evaluating leaders, I have stumbled across a leadership shortcoming that continually amazes me. Leaders will manage a team, work with the same individuals every day, yet hardly know anything about their people! The best leaders are readers of people. They have the intuitive ability to understand others by discerning how they feel and recognizing what they sense."

John Maxwell

Let's face it, managers can quickly get a feel for the atmosphere of their office just by walking around, observing and listening. Doing more with less, chances of layoffs, an emphasis on productivity, and a host of other factors contribute to many employees not even enjoying going to work, much less having fun, being relaxed and feeling valued or productive.

The top three team conflicts:
Communication
Fun versus work
Not doing it right or my way

When is someone actually a leader? Is it supervising, hiring, training or managing others? Doesn't it start with yourself? *Treating others as you want to be treated* is a great saying, but with different personalities, it won't always work. You know if you are a micro-manager, a leader who hates paperwork, or a person of few words that wants to be left alone to get the job done. That is not necessarily the leadership style others want or need. There are many qualities that have made you very successful, but they are quite different for others.

The power and practicality of the Colors seminar gives you the words to put with specific strengths, stresses, feelings and behaviors. But some strengths can also be your weaknesses if you let them. One way is to impose your values on others who don't share them, your approach, or your methods. Should any of the basic challenges for your Color not apply— congratulations. There is a difference between Colors and behaviors, but it always starts with an awareness; a genuine desire to grow and an openness to the valuable strengths other Colors bring to any team, talent pool, customer service and company. When others drive you nuts because they are so different, even a simple mental checklist of many positive traits is a great way to stay mindful of the values and contributions of other Colors to your team and company.

We often take our most talented staff,
take them out of the team and
promote them (or attempt to change them)
to become Gold managers.

On our team:

Orange provides the energy
Green provides the quality
Gold provides the practicality
Blue provides the heart

Leadership Styles and Functions

Leadership styles are always more about preferences than about abilities. Sometimes you need to be a leader and not a manager. One of the differences is that managers do things right— leaders do the right thing. For Gold, the focus is often on the managing part of their job due to their powerful strengths in that area. How does anyone become more of a leader? The first thing is to stop wondering and get going. Start acting, make things happen and create an environment for success with a focus on people and the big picture rather than on the daily tasks and challenges.

After all, success and results are not about tasks, products or sales. They're about service and people – always have been and always will be. Results certainly matter, but relationships matter more. And when relationships deteriorate, sales and results will always decline.

For some Colors, success grows by treating optimism, happiness, and staying positive as skills to be learned (and practiced), instead of a state of mind. Leaders present a clear vision of the future, which creates excitement and drive. See the vision, own it and then communicate it. After that, it is taking the first steps toward staying flexible, patient and determined. Leaders also believe in others when they don't really believe in themselves. Besides, you become successful through an act of will more than skill and people don't experience you as you are but only as they see you.

One of your biggest strengths as a manager is to acknowledge your shortcomings.

Our natural leadership and management style is certainly through using the talents of our primary Color. However, different situations call for different approaches. The natural skills of our Colors can often turn from strengths to weaknesses if they are taken one step too far, or if they are used into a different environment.

In the military, for example, lives can depend on others carrying out your word. Following orders is not optional. It's not about being nice and getting along, and there certainly isn't room for discussion or debate. Yet, if you were to take that same attitude and mindset into your home and with your family, it's likely you wouldn't make it through a weekend without a huge conflict or fight.

Some Major Functions of a Leader:

- communicate a clear vision

- build a real and balanced team which addresses the core needs and motivators of your staff

- keep your tem motivated and focused

- stay flexible in your paths, but not your destination

- find the balance between freedom and responsibility

- focus your energy on building your team members' strengths

- provide appropriate feedback that is meaningful and welcome in the 'language' of someone's personality type

- put the right people & the right talents in the right positions

- maximize your team members' performance

- distribute the workload fairly, evenly and with flexibility to adapt to circumstances as warranted

- keep everyone informed

- invest in your team with your time, talent and training

- stay aware of your staff's Colors and particular strengths, stresses and ways of communicating

Without many of these components, turnover can be a challenge. The vast majority of staff do not quit over money issues. Surveys show that money is generally not one of the top five reasons people leave a company. Compensation often just becomes a substitute or different measuring tool, when employees are not able to get their core needs met.

The particular questions staff ask and the values they look for are outlined extensively in the book *Colorful Personalities – Discover Your Personality Type Through the Power of Colors*. Some of the more common staff values very much revolve around their Colors:

- A larger amount of freedom— often the Orange wording for having flexibility, less paperwork, not being chained to a desk, or a position which allows them more input, creativity or a chance to do it their way.

- Fit in better— the Gold and Blue drive for a strong sense of belonging.

- More teamwork— the Blue description of opportunities and the need to work with others, as well as having closer bonds and the drive to feel more included.

- Appreciation— Orange, through frequently recognition and ability to be paid commissions and bonuses for their efforts, and Gold through tangible and fair ways for always going the extra mile to complete tasks and projects without prompting.

- More chance for input and to improve the process— Green seeking acknowledgement of their ability to improve processes when better ways exist, and to be heard when their best thinking has suggestions and feedback.

What Makes a Great Manager?

First, Break All The Rules is a book by Marcus Buckingham who argues that all talented employees need a great manager who engages his or her employees as the key to successfully managing teams toward excellence in performance.

When the author looked at more than two decades of data, he found that a great manager doesn't actually follow the tried and true. He gives these thoughts:
• people don't change very much
• don't waste your time trying to put in what was left out
• try to draw out what was left in

The tools of Colors will always highlight our unique talents and gifts. They're part of our Colors and are quite different than skills, which can actually be taught. But surveys continue to show that 60 to 80 percent of people are not happy in their jobs. It's not hard to see that they're simply not using their natural talents and gifts.

Recently, a company was on the verge of terminating their top (Orange) sales person because she continually turned in her expense reports months after their due date. But after the Colors training, a high Gold receptionist was given the job of assisting with this paperwork. The receptionist loved being able to help organize the sales lady, and it took her less than five minutes a day! What did it do for the sales person? Her production actually went up when the emphasis was no longer on *retraining* her to do paperwork better.

Another great example is that of Paull Travel in Edmonton, which is reviewed in the *Colorful Personalities* book and is one of the best examples of living and understanding the use of personality types and team building. Owner Lesley

Paull actually has half travel agents and half support staff—something unheard of in her field and thought unsustainable by everyone in the industry.

Radical as it may seem, the agency has continued to enjoy unparalleled growth through some of the most difficult and challenging times in the industry. Her Orange staff can excel at their strengths without the stress of excessive paperwork. Her Gold staff can contribute to travel sales but is allowed to focus on being teamed up with the Orange agents to keep an eye on the details, ticketing specifics and follow-up.

Paull's definition of support staff, however, is not a typical one. All incentives, bonuses, training, gifts and trips always encompass her entire team, regardless of job description or title. "We always do everything together. We don't have two different classes of staff— ever," says Paull.

Another example is of Dean and his partner who own a large fitness chain— a very high Orange business. Fortunately, that's the first Color of both Dean and his partner. An understanding of their personalities has long since required them to hire Steve, a Green controller. He handles banking, finance, legal and all the daily functions that aren't *fun* for most Orange people. Almost every morning Dean would burst into Steve's office with little slips of paper, a virtual waterfall of ideas off the top of his head, and many questions in a typical Orange, rapid-fire approach. It was driving Steve nuts, while Dean was convinced his controller was constantly in a bad mood.

There are times we think we're helping
a different Color, but we're really just
annoying them and stressing them out.

It was after a seminar that it became clear to Dean that his controller's mood was simply caused by his Orange behavior. He perceived his quick questions, rapidly changing tracks, and many Orange ideas as positives, and expected Steve to instantly react and offer feedback. Steve, however, had a tendency to become apprehensive whenever this Orange "tornado" hit his office. Dean had always known the value of his Green controller, but now understood that Steve would only supply feedback and information that was correct, well thought out and justified. He has learned to first communicate with Steve through e-mails, a note, or rattling off his thoughts on voice-mail and then arranging to meet at the end of the day. It wasn't easy, but it created a vastly improved relationship when he allowed his controller to work on his strengths instead of pressing him for *instant* answers.

Isn't there always a big difference between focusing on what our talents and gifts are, and how we can continue to build on them, instead of focusing on what we're not doing well? Great managers focus on their team's primary Colors and build on the things each team member does well. They find a way to change a minor part of the job and have learned to build their staff around the strengths of a well-balanced team consisting of all Colors.

Things can go horribly wrong when you don't understand each other.

Orange Leadership Styles

Orange leaders are very ambitious, energetic and believe in the saying: *'never let them see you sweat.'* They are the least likely to get stressed, with a built-in *'don't worry – be happy'* attitude, and the firm knowledge that there really isn't anything they cannot do or solve. They excel in situations requiring immediate, hands-on action and trouble shooting skills.

Their strong desire for flexibility makes them able to react quickly, think on their feet, adapt to change, feedback, and new information as they go along. In the eyes of an Orange, meetings should never last more than 15 minutes. After all, they're designed to throw out some basic ideas and create the start of a plan. If better information comes along, it will be incorporated and plans easily amended or dropped altogether.

These are definitely energy leaders who are the consummate cheerleaders without micro-managing. A meeting with an Orange can quickly make others think a hurricane has hit their office. As great multi-taskers with so much happening, they have neither the time nor the interest in getting involved in their staff's details, projects or routine decisions. Specifics, worrying about potential pitfalls, written backup, budgeting or schedules are best left to their Gold staff. After all, where is the fun in that— or the payoff for that matter.

As leaders, they simply look for the end product where results speak for themselves. When they are asked for a progress report, it is not something they aren't readily able to supply. Parts of a project are on notes, some is at home, some is in their briefcase (isn't it?) and a lot of it is in their head. After all, this is one of the most creative Color groups. All the pieces are somewhere, but it will take a big push to put them all together — and probably right before the deadline.

They are not a Color to expect much different of their staff, trusting their employees to come through when it counts. No excuses, no whining— just get it done, whatever it takes, no matter what. For updates they prefer a quick overview of the big picture. Others may feel it is cruel to not be supportive in many details along the way, but that's life. It does allow their staff to get sidetracked and have some fun. After all, it's a big part of their life.

A challenge for staff is that Orange can sometimes repeat instructions, or can forget to pass them along altogether. With so much happening, they may well cover something twice, leading staff of some Colors to think they are being treated as dummies. Forgetting to pass on information creates stress for others as well. They meant to, but something else came up. Orange won't beat themselves up over it and cannot see why this would possibly create stress for anyone else.

Orange Leadership Styles

Their position has to be fun, full of variety, involve people and provide constant challenges. They have a great imagination and believe anything is possible. Consistently positive and always on the move, Orange possesses a natural ability to multi-task many projects at once.

This approach is definitely by choice. It is one of the tools they have to avoid boredom at all costs. But it can also easily over-extend them. However, they are able to pick up the pieces where they left off and always keep five or six things moving forward with ease and little stress. Their door is always open, they are more than willing to get sidetracked for a while, and always have time for their staff, or anyone dropping by. These are welcome distractions as all of them involve people who help take them away from the curse of paperwork.

The ability to multi-task can also cause panic or stress for other who need preparation and organization. After all, it can mean a sudden change in plans, last minute ideas, or over-looking some of the details.

With their strong sense of impatience and creativity, it is a Color that knows how to get things done quickly or knows who to call for help. Orange has a great networking skill and has no hesitation in asking for input instead of struggling through issues. Results always speak louder than words, and the end often justifies the means.

They won't back down from any challenge and are great motivators. Others might not think something is reasonable, but that doesn't matter— suck it up and get on with it. They are highly allergic to whiners and negative people and will quickly let it show since it is difficult for Orange to understand how other Colors can have such a different attitude.

Anything negative or staff worrying about obstacles and problems, drives them crazy. They're quite patient with staff for a while, and the first jabs will be humorous, but inside they're going out of their mind. Their bluntness can easily hurt the feelings of staff. The niceties and handholding will often have to wait— right now there is a job to get done and they have too much happening to notice hurt feelings. But then their natural gift and sense of humor with people will quickly be able to smooth things over later.

Their creativity and constant can-do attitude has Orange leaders starting many more projects than they could ever hope to finish. Wanting to win, their ability to adapt, and being flexible means lots of their ideas or projects can get dropped, passed on to their staff or quickly amended as needed. Changing tracks or getting bored with something are natural traits for Orange leaders.

When they're down, they'll be way down. It does not happen very often since they use their great sense of humor to hide almost all their pain and hurt feelings. This state of mind occurs frequently when upper management

Orange Leadership Styles

17

starts to impose more structure and rules or handcuff their Orange leaders from functioning in their own way. In those cases, others will certainly hear about it.

A common example comes about when Gold senior management micro-manages them, or focuses on small challenges without relevance to the big picture. Another example is when Orange is asked to do written goal statements and the like. Not only are they far superior at verbal skills, they also would much rather proceed as things come at them without being stuck, or fixed, to a specific operating plan. Those are common situations when Orange want to vote with their feet— '*take this job and shove it*,' as the song says.

Orange knows they can handle any problem easier than anyone else. Plus they will linger over poor results for a much shorter period of time. After all, they live in the present, without much of a rear-view mirror to second-guess decisions or beat themselves up over past issues. Orange dusts themselves off, learns their lesson and moves forward without missing a step, or losing their optimism.

Orange leaders demand loyalty and can be unsympathetic to some of the needs of their team. Since they require little down time, it is sometimes frustrating that others don't share their drive. It also means they have limited tolerance for mistakes. After all, winning is everything, and often all-consuming, where many things can be justified to achieve results.

Their impatience can also show through by interrupting others, finishing their sentences, or jumping in to supply an answer— any answer— just to get on with it! They may become bored quickly with details, paperwork or meetings, which can lead to overlooking the finer points of a presentation or project. However, they are very results-oriented and really need their team to get to the point and not waste their time.

As leaders, they inspire others by living the saying: '*Don't take yourself so seriously.*' They are natural charmers with an ability to turn problems into positives. They are almost the circus masters who make the office fun and inspire others through their energy, quick thinking, flexibility and drive to win at almost any price. They live for compliments and certainly won't hold a grudge.

Orange Leadership Styles

The world sees 35 feet and thinks, "There's no way." They see it and think, "Start engraving the trophy."
PGA Tour Ad

Gold Leadership Styles

Gold leaders are the group that gets the job done (as the profile story on page 38 shows so well). They prefer to do one thing at a time, do it very well, and then move on. They are very conscientious and ethical, always doing things right and maintaining consistently high standards. As the largest Color group in the population, they are also the largest number of managers. Golds are a steady, stabilizing influence, providing structure, tradition and focus wherever they go. Plus, they are highly talented in administration and logistics and are also the hardest working group.

Their main strengths consist of designing detailed and practical ways to allocate resources and talents to the appropriate people, job or situation at just the right time. It will be done efficiently, cost-effectively, and with no chance of overlooking any detail, or leaving any stone unturned. They operate within the framework, rules and policies in place, and unless these are changed, Gold leaders do not feel it is their place to reinvent the wheel or vary from current procedures.

Gold leaders are very hard on themselves. They are consumed with a drive to make it accurate, right or perfect— nothing less will do for themselves and they frequently run with significant stress levels. So it's natural that they expect this of their staff as well. To others this can be seen as nitpicking and micromanaging, which often leads to resentment. Their outlook is one of concern, with an eye on potential pitfalls, loose ends, upcoming speed bumps and possible errors. It can certainly get others to start questioning their perceived value, which can be a double-edged sword. Gold leaders are trusted and efficient and give very few reasons to question any of their decisions, motives or planning. Unfortunately it can make them hard on their staff. They expect nothing less of others than they are prepared to do themselves.

Just a simple issue of reviewing their department or company financial statement will quickly show this. Revenue is over forecast, but two of 50 expense items are slightly over budget. For many, this is a great reason to celebrate. Not so for most Gold who focus on the two problems where their performance is clearly not up to par. It might be an area of little significance, but that's not the point. Questions need to be asked, details reviewed and a plan formulated to fix it. It is definitely not something they wish to see repeated ever again. Certainly this is a simple example that shows their huge value to senior management.

On the other side, putting that same focus on their staff can quickly create resentment as staff can feel inadequate. One of the biggest challenges staff has is with the Gold focus on the negative issues that are often perceived as being blown out of proportion.

Yet this is also a group that recognizes achievements in clear, fair and measurable ways. They will convey them through tangible tokens of thanks more than personal appreciation. However, the Gold leaders often wonder if their talents are really appreciated. They wonder if others even notice all the times they go over and above what is asked of them with no fanfare or desire for attention. Something has to get done, they gave their word and it will be accomplished, no matter what. It is really only Gold senior managers or their Gold staff who truly understand what efforts and work go into their day. Therefore, Gold values recognition— even if they are really bad in accepting compliments. More often than not, they dismiss them, downplay their efforts, or pass them onto their team and others, while secretly very much appreciating them.

Gold leaders are very loyal to both their company and their staff and will defend both against outside forces. When negative feedback needs to be shared, it is done behind closed doors and in private. The outside world should never see disagreements or challenges, as they'll reflect poorly on them, their staff, and the status and reputation of the company. With their staff, Gold leaders are also very attentive listeners who are never sidetracked, and they quickly become the stabilizers to their team and keep everyone out of chaos.

One of the primary drives for every Gold leader is to make well thought-out decisions which consider all the details and possibilities before executing the plan. They are practical and look for realistic goals, not lofty dreams. Reports will always include all these details and specifics. It is what they need, so naturally they will supply it to others. They want things done properly— even if they often have to step in and do it themselves.

Gold leaders understand they will be judged on performance and assure that no stone is left unturned to get it done right. The proper framework, organization and plan allow the successful completion of almost anything they take on. Hence, a large part of their initial work will revolve around these areas. Gold wouldn't be comfortable starting a job without having these organizational pillars in place.

For Gold, anything can be done if it is first planned and outlined before jumping into action. It is their method in almost all areas of their life. It simply assures them that the structure is set and nothing needs to be re-visited, re-done or changed in the future.

Golds can be counted on to stay on schedule and keep their promises. After all, their word is their bond in all areas of their life, and employees can count on them to always keep it, even when it is no longer expedient. They will not deviate from a game plan or decision, and outside distractions will not keep them from achieving their objectives. They tend to be perfectionists and expect it of their staff as well as themselves.

Gold leaders are focused and business-like. To others they might seem reserved and cool at times, but that's not the case at all. Fun and socializing are important— but meant for after work. Right now there is a job to get done and many more things to complete on their to-do list before anyone should relax. Plus, they strongly value their privacy and a distinct line between their personal life and career. Gold are extremely devoted to their company as well as their small group of friends and family. But to people they work with, Gold can seem withdrawn or certainly hard to get to know. Any Gold leader will seldom share many personal stories with their team.

Gold leaders value their stability, traditions and tried and true methods. They tend to view most issues as black or white. Staff never have a problem understanding when they're out of line. It is very clear that rules and policies need to be followed. After all, they create safety and a structured operating framework which allows everyone to pull in the same direction.

Deviating from the norm is something that is out of the Gold comfort zone and only reluctantly done since they are cautious decision-makers who value controlling their environment. It can also cause Gold leaders not to be immediately receptive to new ideas or unproven methods.

Office gossip sometimes says the only good idea is one coming from their Gold boss.

While that may be the perception, Gold leaders are more than ready to listen to suggestions and improvements. Just don't expect them to be implemented starting tomorrow. While they can quickly dismiss them, in most cases they will want time to think them through, weigh the options and consequences and consider the ramifications of any changes.

The Gold group is very loyal (to a fault) and very concerned about their staff. They will readily step in to help and clean up after others — in more ways than one. They will always be willing to pitch in where needed since any self-sacrifice to accomplish their goals will be done without a fuss. But they can be quite introspective as well.

Gold tends to have deep running feelings and often take disagreements quite personally. That may make them appear difficult to please, but all in all, when something needs to get done, irrespective of the challenges and obstacles, a Gold leader will always come through— on time, on budget and as promised— always.

It may not be flashy, but it is substantive. Besides, doesn't methodical and steady generally win the race?

*Golds hate catch and release
management decision-making:
"We'd made that decision already,
but here it is again swimming around!"*

Green Leadership Styles

The greatest strengths of Green leaders are their exceptional talents for strategic planning and detailed goal setting. They have a strong ability to work with complex systems which require a great deal of thought, research skills and lateral thinking. Their calm manner is important in many situations and crises, but can also act as a double-edged sword. After a certain amount of time on a project, for better or worse, they will easily pass the routine tasks to others and can show some impatience with trivial details. In the meantime, they are looking for something— anything more challenging.

There really isn't a problem or question they wouldn't want to tackle. Green continuously evaluates, probes, challenges, searches and seeks better ways of improving systems. It is almost as though they are playing a game with themselves to find better ways, more efficient production methods or a range of other improvements that utilize their great skills.

After all, Green leaders are very attracted to theoretical analysis, and are the group who challenges the rest of the Colors to raise their consciousness of how the world could be, instead of settling for the status-quo.

Part of that means others will have to be ready for the ever-present 'why' questions. It is their effort to challenge conventional wisdom, to probe and to learn. Without a strong sense of self-confidence, or a well-researched position, others can find themselves in over their head. But from this Color, questioning is not meant as criticism. It is almost always communicating better information. When others understand this, it creates a significantly different mindset and demeanor. Knowing this makes their Green leaders or managers a great resource for information, options and feedback.

The mindset of Green is to supply the correct answer, not just any answer, and to respond when they are ready and on their timetable. The more complex, the less likely it is that there will be a quick response. Green leaders are driven to get it right and not just to get it done, so they will readily go away to think things through. This gives them the chance to process all information and analyze their options. It is not, as others often wonder, anything they did wrong, or being anti-social. This can also make them seem unapproachable or aloof, which is not the case, although they are often a difficult Color to connect with. Small talk and idle chit-chat are of no interest to Green, as they are people of few words. Added to that is their large vocabulary and often neutral expression.

The drive to do it right and say it correctly comes from the strong Green need for credibility. On their part, it shows in the drive to think it through before talking, research the issue before committing and even assuring that their e-mails are spell-checked and grammatically correct before pressing the send button. When they find these same traits in others, Green will allow those people a generous amount of freedom and flexibility as a result. But in anyone dealing with them (as the book *The Colors of Sales and Customers* explains in detail), Green tolerates absolutely no lying or bluffing.

In conversations with Green leaders, others often make the mistake of looking to the 93 percent of communication that is non-verbal. For them, communication is not an active banter back and forth. Unfortunately, that can lead their team to feel they are not being heard. Nothing could be further from the truth. The Green mental computer is on and their notebooks are open— they're often better listeners than other Colors, but it will not be in an active manner.

Their huge strength lies in their joy of learning and teaching. Learning about anything and everything, teaching then becomes payday for Green. The chance to pass information on to others and watch them utilize these tools is a great self-esteem builder. They excel at taking concepts, problems or situations, and bringing them to a manageable size that their team won't find overwhelming. They will easily grasp what needs to be done and find solutions based on the best information available.

They are strong leaders who are constantly moving forward, perfecting and finding many solutions before anyone else. That makes them self-sufficient and born leaders. It also makes it very hard to move them off an opinion or a position when they clearly know they have a better way and have all the research to back it up. No emotional outburst, no state of depression, or high fives, just calm, cool and collected— as always. To staff, it can appear that they are not excited or enthusiastic, or come across as having a *'better than us'* outlook.

Tough, unfeeling, sarcastic, or not caring about people, are words staff sometimes use behind their back. While that may sound cruel, Green does acknowledge that one of their stresses is being asked to repeat themselves over and over. After all, it isn't logical for staff to need constant acknowledgement, recognition and reassurance. They know they are valued and appreciated, and any Green leader will certainly let them know when it changes. Until then, previous information stands.

Most Green leaders tend to be introverts with a preference of dealing with facts over feelings. When faced with achieving an objective, they have a single-minded focus and drive with no end to their commitment of time and energy. When that happens, tensing under stress, setting unrealistic standards, and missing meals can easily happen.

What they do enjoy is a good debate or argument with anyone — about almost any subject as long as the other person has the smarts to put up a good fight. Besides, they're very self-confident and love to be challenged and tested. What they do not appreciate is having their thought process questioned. That necessitates asking properly worded questions, since there is a measurable difference between asking *'have you considered this'* and a much more neutral *'would this work?'* phrasing.

It is also wise to avoid any perceived signs of stupidity, as they view it. Stupid meetings that push for closure without sufficient information, stupid rules when there is clearly a better way, and stupid questions will quickly have them show their impatience, a sarcastic comment, or a very recognizable non-verbal facial expression.

"You people are telling me what you think I want to know. I want to know what is actually happening."
Creighton Abrams

Blue Leadership Styles

Blue leaders are the glue that keeps a team working together as a group. With their unique ways everyone will feel included and know they are valuable and cared about. They excel in diplomacy and personal relationships. One of their primary drives is that an office function in an inclusive manner where opinions count and success is a team effort. Blue views their leadership role as building a democratic climate and collaborative model where everyone contributes, grow, and learns together, and they are always open to new ideas.

Blue inspires their staff and firmly believe that everyone is equal and will become successful under his or her leadership, each in their unique way. They actually do care and are quite attuned to the social needs of their staff. They also have a drive to build relationships and to support others in achieving success and their dreams. This includes making sure things are OK in their personal life as well as their work life, being amongst the first to host social functions and to celebrate birthdays — anything to strengthen the bonds of their group.

A strong desire to maintain peace at all cost means others can get frustrated with them, partly because it is very hard to be mad at a Blue manager who seeks to have harmony without disagreement. One of their biggest stresses is terminating anyone and giving reviews or negative feedback to a staff member. A primary drive is to be liked and to avoid confrontation or hurt feelings whenever possible. Negative feedback hurts them as much as the person they are dealing with. Besides, they really do feel that part of it has to be their fault. Not to mention, they will feel extremely badly, and often for many days.

Blue leaders and managers are definitely diplomats who know just what to say and how to say it. These skills make them excellent interviewers who listen actively and with great sympathy so others feel attended to and supported. They are always available, with an open mind, no matter what the reason or timing. Blue leaders know the priority is people, without question. Of course, this can cause them to quite often run late when someone needs to talk, but also makes it possible to always see them without notice or an appointment. If someone wants to catch them— the paperwork can always wait.

With their patience, Blue leaders are also great trainers who are receptive to ideas and suggestions. What they do consider first is the effect on their staff over procedural fixes or improvements. This openness makes any Blue an excellent motivator. With their positive demeanor and gentle nudging, others readily see and feel that this person genuinely cares, wants them to succeed and will help them accomplish their goals. What a wonderful success for any Blue whose drive is to make a small difference in the life of others.

It is easy to see that they are a very expressive group. One-word answers are a large clue that something is wrong. They won't come out and say what is bothering them in order to avoid feeling selfish by discussing their problem, instead of helping someone else.

To others, Blue leaders can come across as undisciplined and at times lacking focus. Not wanting to make waves, they can also become very quiet or withdrawn. Their desire to look for the good in others can also be a turn-off to staff that may judge much quicker when someone should be disciplined or dealt with. As managers, they also have the typical Blue inability to say 'no,' causing them to frequently give in to others, or be taken advantage of. That can become very draining and frequently causes them to get run down. After all, it's all about accommodating others over their own needs. When Blue reaches this stage, it creates a general view that they have not done enough and could have or should have done more.

Blue leaders are very easy going. They don't get upset easily and have an uncanny ability to put a positive spin on any issue or situation. To their team it may seem unrealistic, but Blue will be undeterred. In fact, at times they appear to have selective hearing to filter out negatives, confrontational issues or challenges that do not fit their mindset of staying positive, people or team oriented and customer driven. It is not something others readily understand and certainly cannot measure. But it serves Blue leaders well when they follow their instinct and intuition.

They do remember most negatives and their feelings are easily hurt. In those situations, Blue will forgive but never forget. In fact, they won't even come out and tell someone when their feelings have been hurt, as that would just appear selfish. An apology is fine, but what their staff of other Colors will not know is that only the Blue is the final judge and jury of deciding whether they feel the apology was genuine, sincere and acceptable.

When it comes to problem solving, Blue have the creativity and ability to think outside the box. If solutions need to be found, you can bet on a Blue finding a win-win answer that others will embrace. Now if they could only convince their Gold and Green senior management that their people skills are just as important as the tasks to be completed, everyone would get along so much better.

"I don't do great things.
I do small things with great passion."
Mother Teresa

Gold and Green are 'task first' Colors who differ in the methods with which things gets done, or are made right and perfect. Both function through logical ways of accomplishing goals, but differ in their priorities and approach to projects and challenges. Both want to understand and master things, and tend to talk about facts and specifics. This is an attitude of questioning, probing, plus looking for pitfalls and loose ends. Both relate today's problem solving to past experience with a methodical approach and an aversion to being sidetracked or interrupted. They function in the here and now, living life in realistic terms, while focusing on challenges or specifics and avoiding generalizations. They communicate in a direct manner which often does not consider the tactfulness or implication of comments. This can lead to hurt feelings but they often don't see it at all.

When it comes to picking up clues around them, Gold and Green generally need to be told directly, as both have challenges on picking up non-verbal clues. Their personality makes both good quality managers who are independent in their decision making. They make the hard choices, but if the question is *would you rather be happy or right?* — right is quite important, and often the case. In society, the majority of men tend to be Gold and Green. Conflict can be more common, but is also resolved quicker. Both might have an all-out disagreement or argument, but quickly move past it and settle their issues.

Blue and Orange are 'people' Colors and relationships-first personality types. Both understand life is a journey to live and learn along the way while always building connections with others. They do this by using their optimism, positive outlook and dreams. Both work well in teams and situations where verbal skills take priority over written material. Blue and Orange can show their lack of enthusiasm when too many routine tasks are involved — even more so if they are isolated from interacting with others. These two Colors consider people in their decision making and prefer to work in harmony and teams, using their social ability and humor. They choose to make decisions by consensus and develop plans and ideas with feedback from others. As a result, both are flexible in changing decisions when better information comes along.

They value positive feedback and recognition. Orange will never be shy about it, while Blue will often deflect the recognition to others. However, inside they are very happy to be recognized— especially for their unique talents and contribution. Blue and Orange can tell by someone's face if and when something is wrong or not working. As they are quite instinctive, both Colors are very good at reading people and use the 93 percent of communication that is non-verbal to pick up clues and signals. These two are also very collaborative and excellent leaders with their creativity and flexibility.

How Are You Doing?

A large part of any leadership and management position is to provide feedback to staff in many ways, and on various levels. Different Color groups have their own challenges in either wanting to do it at all, or the methods and tools for making it effective and win-win. Four main points for feedback should include:

- Providing information, not opinions. It is a lot harder to stay factual, but also much more valuable.

- Know what to say and when to say it. There is a significant difference between feedback on an initial outline or a final presentation.

- Don't hold back any positive things to say. This leaves the door open to be sought out openly and freely again along the way and in the future. At the same time it shows that you are paying attention and looking for the value, which greatly contributes to reducing stress levels for staff. Positive comments will allow staff to buy into your constructive feedback and feel better about adopting it.

- Don't avoid feedback as it creates a win-win and should be a positive experience to honor staff by allowing them to know when they are on-track.

A Gold Management Insight

As the largest group in the population, and the people who value being behind the scenes rather than in the spotlight, vast numbers of high Gold people are invaluable as managers in almost every company of any size.

One of the most misunderstood things about the Gold management style can come when things get off track, deadlines are approaching or the time has come to get on with something. And nothing describes this more clearly than the following story:

"Hurray For Honore!" That was the comment by CNN anchor Miles O'Brien, when the U.S. government put very high Gold Three Star Lt.-General Russel Honore in charge of the horrific situation in New Orleans in the aftermath of Hurricane Katrina. Day four brought the first pictures, comments and actions by Honore, and almost all media outlets immediately realized and commented, that things had indeed, turned around.

Before then, management coordination was shaky at best. In fact, on day two, 300 ambulances wanted to get into New Orleans from Florida, but were told they hadn't been asked for and needed state permission and FEMA authorization before rolling. They never did turn a wheel when nobody felt they had the authority (or perhaps will) to make it happen.

While it's speculations, you can bet that Honore first asked whether he'd have the resources, power and freedom to get things done his way. After all, Gold usually won't step up or volunteer without knowing they'll have the tools to be successful. They generally won't rev it up until they know there will be at least an even-money chance of success. In the case of Honore, that included a direct line to President Bush, something he certainly didn't hesitate to use.

After a few minutes of television coverage, it became obvious that this Lt. General was a very high Gold (nothing surprising, as it's the largest group of officers). Direct and blunt questions, comments, and orders, along with a total focus on what needs to be done now, and zero tolerance of delays, obstacles, or politics, all proved this obvious personality type.

CNN anchor Tony Harris described it as "a rough voice, an even rougher manner, and someone who tolerates no excuse." (Yup, that's Gold.) One of the Lt. General's first orders was to redirect helicopters to a hospital. When that hadn't started 20 minutes later, Honore went ballistic. He also continued to re-focus people (mostly politicians) onto specific tasks with a clear mission of getting whatever priority off the to-do list and moving on. This included hands-on work, as Golds stay involved to make things happen and to ensure that their orders and directions are carried out. After all, few things are more valuable to high Gold than being able to cross things off their to-do lists in order to achieve a great sense of accomplishment and be able to move on. Besides, their impatience would never allow them to sit in an office away from the action. In the case of Honore, his command posts for the first few days were the street corners in various parishes of New Orleans.

Every office has been in a situation where a high Gold has stepped forward for one reason or another. Without an understanding of Colors, most people might have serious reservations, or judgments, of what was happening at the time.

In many similar circumstances (well, nothing compares to the four hurricane-affected States), Gold leaders are not politically correct, not overly concerned with feelings, or interested in hearing about obstacles. They'll have little time or interest in meetings, excuses, or anyone's lack of focus and discipline on specific tasks, to see things through to completion.

Is this the most popular way to get something done? Never. Is there a time and circumstance when this type of management style is necessary? You decide. But for the people of New Orleans, the answer was clear.

Gold can, at times, have a management style that is difficult for other Colors to understand or appreciate. They are fiercely protective and loyal to their company and staff and often, without advertising it, can put their careers on the line for their team. To most who are Gold, it's the right thing to do, and when they believe they're right, few things will dissuade them.

Gold are also very sensitive to criticism, which they take very hard and find difficult to understand. Yes, they are very caring and sensitive to the feelings of others. But it shows in unique and special Gold ways that others need to understand through the insights of Colors.

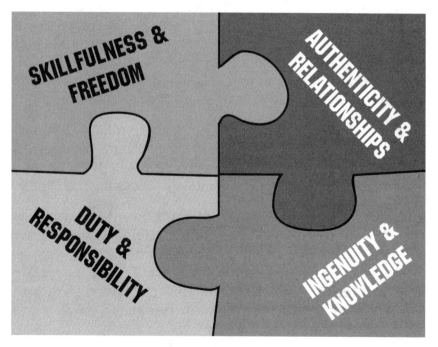

Are You Running the Meeting?

For any staff meeting or training session, here are some things that each Color group looks for:

Orange values:

- focusing on *now* and immediate plans, goals and actions
- practicality – what's in it for me
- visuals
- exercises
- fast paced and clever
- frequent breaks (or keep it short)
- getting to the point
- varied materials
- a sense of humor
- a flexible schedule or facilitator
- the chance to get involved
- ability to talk it through vs. needing the perfect thing said first
- taking it easy on handouts and paperwork
- not making me read a bunch of stuff before or at the meeting – I won't
- telling me what you want done and get on with it
- reminding me about the meeting

Gold values:

- adequate notice
- an outline or agenda in advance
- testimonials
- examples
- handouts and written material
- links to what exists now
- practical benefits
- realistic goals and outcomes
- time-line adhered to by facilitator (or agenda)
- to be left alone (not put on the spot), to just listen
- staying on track, on-task and on the subject
- not covering topics that should be sent by e-mail
- not wasting time by repeating information
- not re-visiting previous decisions
- ending the meeting on time, as promised
- stating specific expectations of what needs to be done
- not leaving any loose ends to discuss again later

Green values:

- an organized meeting
- logical plans, presentations or suggestions
- concrete solutions
- big picture outline first
- innovative ideas and lateral thinking
- answers to the "why" questions
- testimonials
- independent thinking/processing time
- resources on the web

- credibility of the chair or facilitator and content
- the material in advance so I can be pro-active
- keeping the noise level down
- one person talks at a time
- not being put on the spot – I'll let you know when I've thought it through
- a proper summary and wrap-up
- chance to supply input by e-mail at a later time
- logical, credible and pertinent materials, handouts or background information

Blue values:
- feelings-oriented
- new possibilities
- cover any impact or effect on people and my team
- humor and warmth
- enthusiasm
- uplifting and positive
- assurance that everyone feels included
- small group work when possible
- a comfortable setting
- listening to me when I share
- a genuine facilitator or manager running the meeting
- eye contact & acknowledge me
- allow everyone to participate and be heard
- sharing time afterwards
- not getting too hung up on an agenda
- never running down my ideas or feedback
- listening to what I'm not saying

Successful Leaders and Teams Share:

Common goals	Gold
Curiosity	Green
Cooperation	Blue
Creativity	Orange
Cost-cutting skills	Gold
Courage	Green
Commitment	Gold
Connecting with teammates	Blue
Can-do attitude	Orange
Cementing relationships	Blue
Continuity	Gold
Cheerful no-worries attitude	Orange
Certainty	Green
Customer retention	Blue
Conscientious	Gold
Change acceptance	Orange
Caring	Blue
Character	Gold
Coaching skills	Green
Charitable	Blue
Crisis management skills	Orange
Consistency	Gold
Closing instincts	Orange
Credibility	Green
Compromising	Blue
Clutch decision making	Orange
Competence	Green

Common bonds **...that's everyone's
challenge...**

Order Form

#	Title	Investment per	Total amount
____	Colorful Personalities – Discover Your Personality Type Through the Power of Colors	$19.95	_____
____	Colorful Personalities – Audio CD	$9.95	_____
____	The Colors of Leadership & Mgmt.	$6.95	_____
____	The Colors of Parent & Child Dynamics	$6.95	_____
____	The Colors of Sales & Customers	$6.95	_____
____	The Colors of Relationships	$6.95	_____
____	Colors Tools for Christians	$6.95	_____
____	It's Your Money! Tools, Tips and Tricks to Borrow Smarter and Pay It Off Quicker	US Edition: US $14.95 Can. Edition: CAD $19.95 Span. Edition: US $ 6.95	_____ _____ _____
	Tax & shipping (flat amount)		**$ 4.00**
	Total amount:		_____

Name: _____

Address: _____

City: _____ Pr./St.: _____ PC/Zip: _____

E-mail: _____

Payment enclosed by: ____check   ____cash   ____money order

Or Visa/MC: _____/_____/_____/_____   Exp date:____/____

Order by: Fax: (780) 432 5613 Web: www.yourmoneybook.com
E-mail: george@vantageseminars.com
Mail: Canada: Box 4080 Edmonton, AB, T6E 4S8
US: 14781 Memorial Dr. #1183 Houston, TX 77079